——NEED FOR GOD IN——
HUMAN
SOCIETY

NEED FOR GOD IN
HUMAN SOCIETY

JOSEPH BOROWITZ

Library of Congress Control Number: 2017907293
ISBN: Hardcover   978-1-5434-2228-3
                 Softcover   978-1-5434-2227-6
                 eBook   978-1-5434-2226-9

NLT
Scripture quotations marked NLT are taken from the Holy Bible, New Living Translation, copyright © 1996, 2004, 2007. Used by permission of Tyndale House Publishers, Inc. Carol Stream, Illinois 60188. All rights reserved. Website

NKJV
Scripture quotations marked NKJV are taken from the New King James Version. Copyright © 1982 by Thomas Nelson, Inc. Used by permission. All rights reserved.

KJV
Scripture quotations marked KJV are from the Holy Bible, King James Version (Authorized Version). First published in 1611. Quoted from the KJV Classic Reference Bible, Copyright © 1983 by The Zondervan Corporation.

Print information available on the last page.

Rev. date: 05/10/2017

To order additional copies of this book, contact:
Xlibris
1-888-795-4274
www.Xlibris.com
Orders@Xlibris.com
759668

CONTENTS

Preface vii

Chapter 1   God as an Intimate Member of Human

                   Society.. 1

Chapter 2   Our Eternal Destiny 9

Chapter 3   God in Early Development of Human

                   Civilization....................................... 13

Chapter 4   Church and State...19

Chapter 5   Examples of How a Deep Experience with

                   God Can Change Lives...................................... 33

Chapter 6   Nature of Dialogue Between Human Beings 43

Chapter 7   Vitality of Small Prayer Groups 53

Chapter 8   Sunday School as A Small Prayer Group 59

Chapter 9   Families, Prayer, Faith and Healing 63

Chapter 10   Christianity and Pharmacy 75

Chapter 11   Drug Abuse, Society and Religion 81

Chapter 12   Mental Illness as A Disturbance in Society 87

Chapter 13   Conclusion 95

Index..101

At the touch of love, everyone becomes a poet.
—Plato

IDEALLY, ALL GOVERNING bodies must promote peace and concord for every human being who inhabits this world of ours. Anything that deviates from this holy purpose, whether it is a religion or a form of government, must be modified for conformity or eliminated. Furthermore, to foster peace in our world, religions and governments must work hand in hand to promote justice and fairness throughout the world.

The absolute need for God in our societies is evidenced by the great tragedies of godless communism in Russia where twenty million people were killed and in China where eighty million died. Religion is not opium for the people but an essential ingredient if we are to function well as civilized societies.

Who should decide what will promote peace and concord in our world? Should it be individual human beings with all their selfish motives and greed? No, of course not. We all need some guidance and direction by a higher power. We also need a balanced government with divided political powers that can agree on godly principles to guide us into peace and prosperity. Virtues should abound in a good society. The Christian theological virtues of faith, hope, and charity as well as the natural cardinal virtues of prudence, fortitude, temperance, and justice should be plentiful in a well-ordered civilization. May the good Lord guide us closely.

Most Americans (95 percent) believe in God, and 57 percent pray every day (D. Sulmacy. *The Healer's Calling*. Mahwah, New Jersey: Paulist Press, 1997). I believe people in other nations of the world are similar in recognizing and respecting a higher power.

Society and personal experience tell us that our abilities are limited but belief in a higher power helps us to succeed and to benefit ourselves and the world we live in. The Bible says in Matthew 19:26, "With God all things are possible."

Ultimately God's laws should be our guide. People have long studied godly wisdom and have formulated many guidelines for effective lifestyles that would benefit everyone in the world. Why can't we agree on godly principles that would lead this world to peace and prosperity for everyone? War is not the answer. It only leads to destruction and loss of lives. Some argue that a just "defensive" war is the only way to deal with persistent atrocities. May God show us a better way.

JOSEPH BOROWITZ

People must learn to communicate effectively to coordinate world governance. Thus we included a chapter on transactional analysis, which explains how people talk to one another.

Obviously, good relationships are important in human interactions, so a discussion of normal and abnormal factors in personality makeup is also included in this book.

A primary motivation for writing this book was to point out that God is most evident in small prayer groups—people led by the Holy Spirit, people who love one another and meet regularly to worship their almighty, loving Father. Such groups enhance the quality of life in churches, in communities, in cities, and in nations throughout the world.

CHAPTER 1

God as an Intimate Member of Human Society

The greatest question of our time is not communism verses individuality; nor Europe verses America; not even East verses West. It is whether man can survive without God.—Will Durant

Only a fool despises discipline; whoever learns from correction is wise.—Proverbs 15:5

IT IS ESTIMATED that one third of the people who have died in this world of ours have died at the hands of other human beings. We humans are generally not able to live our lives successfully on our own. We need help. That's why religions are so pervasive in all our societies. Churches abound in all countries of the world. I visited Prague, Czech Republic, and found churches on nearly every street corner.

It's not just a church building or the people in the church, the real power there is God Himself, a supernatural being who is truly in control of each of our lives. Our main job in life is to stay related to Him. One meaning of the word *religion* favored by Saint Augustine is "to reconnect" (religare in Latin). It is only when we drift away from God that we have real problems. There was a time in my life when I blamed God for all my difficulties and stopped going to church. It was a very unhappy experience.

How can anyone believe in God when grossly evil things like the Holocaust occur, when millions of innocent people are systematically slaughtered? And the process continues with abortion of nearly sixty million babies in the USA. Where is God in all this? Does the presence of evil prove that God does not exist? No. Evil has been in the world from the time of Adam and Eve; we've had wars, the Holocaust, slavery, abortion, etc. Evil also exists in each one of us. However, Christians believe that the sufferings of Christ on the cross have atoned for and will continue to atone for evil manifested in the world. The Bible says over and over that God will never forsake us. He will always be with us, and He takes care of His chosen people. This is true, but only when we try to be holy people and try to build God's kingdom here on earth; only then will God take care of us and not forsake us.

I have a good friend who is a holy and knowledgeable yet humble person. He confessed that without his faith in Jesus, his life would be a mess. He would be into all kinds of corruption, including lust, dishonesty, jealousy, and pride. Only by staying close to Jesus Christ is he able to lead an

JOSEPH BOROWITZ

honorable and productive life. I was amazed by what he said. I thought he naturally was a strong and holy person. He is highly respected by all who know him and is a strong Christian witness to the whole Purdue campus. But even he must plead with Jesus on a daily basis for guidance and protection.

According to Wikipedia, the real reason for creation is that God wants a free will, loving relationship with each one of us. Prior to creation there was only God, timeless and alone. But His greatest yearning was for connection, for loving relationships. Thus He allowed the big bang to occur, and the universe was set in motion with the purpose of creating human beings who could experience true love and have a loving relationship with God and with each other.

In order to have valid loving relationships, God knew there must be free will because a programmed or coerced person cannot experience true love. Free will then is a universal constant built into the fabric of creation like gravity and the speed of light. We must have free will to either choose love or choose indifference and hatred. So while the world may seem unfair, it must be exactly as it is for loving relationships to emerge.

Some people think that it was not necessary for Jesus to die on the cross for our sins. God is all powerful and could just forgive us because He is so benevolent, and didn't have to allow His Son to die as atonement for our wrongdoings. After all, the New Testament God is a God of love and gentleness as Jesus demonstrated when He walked the earth.

But God knew that in giving humans free will, many would choose to do wrong. He needed to do something dramatic to emphasize the absolute requirement that we follow His ways and be holy as He is holy. So before the world began, He decided to show how much He loves us by sending His Son to the earth and allowing evil men to put Him to death. Although some theologians deny God the Father has feelings, I believe the crucifixion was no fun for God the Father either. He suffered too. So the whole story of Christ on earth (Paschal mystery) was a dramatic demonstration of His love for us.

In Ephesians 4:30, the Bible says, "Do not grieve the Holy Spirit of God by whom you were sealed for the day of redemption." So God the Holy Spirit is a person and can be grieved and has feelings and emotions. Also Psalm 78 says that the people of Israel tested and provoked God with carved images. We were made in God's image, so He may have feelings similar to ours. However, His strongest emotion is love.

So God's love for Jesus is enormous, and to see Him go through the passion and agony on the cross was extremely painful for God the Father. But God knew He had to allow it to happen to show us the importance of leading holy lives and how serious we have to be to in following the example of Jesus. God the Father showed us how much He loves us by permitting the crucifixion of Jesus.

Elie Wiesel was a prisoner and survivor of Auschwitz, the infamous death camp established by the Nazis in World War II. He wrote fifty-seven books and was a professor at Boston University. He has delivered a powerful message of peace, atonement, and human dignity to mankind and received a Nobel Peace Prize in 1986. He summarized his experience at Auschwitz with the statement that "After the Holocaust, I did not lose faith in God, I lost faith in humanity."

John Guandolo is a former FBI agent in the USA who was relieved from his position by Obama officials. He is an expert on radical terrorism and has dealt with many terrorists. In a public presentation in the year 2015, he mentioned that Islam motivates some terrorists. Over and over in the Koran, it says, "Kill the infidel." If people do not convert to Mohammedanism, they should be killed. It seems to me that this must be erased from the Koran in the interest of world peace. The threat of death cannot achieve true love or peace in our world.

When I audited courses in Holy Scripture at Purdue University, Professor Art Zanonni mentioned that it took many hundreds of years for men to understand and appreciate this God of ours. The Old Testament is an immature impression of God. God does not become angry and kill people. The New Testament is a fuller and more accurate description. Jesus said, not "An eye for an eye or a tooth for a tooth," but "Forgive and love one another." However there is evil in this world, and if we are not close to God, He cannot provide His protection and bad things can happen. Faith is the only connecting link by which we make contact with God. Unbelief cuts us off from God.

We may be mad at God for the Holocaust, widespread abortion, or other human tragedies, but if we agree that humanity must have free will, we have to realize that some people will choose evil. However, we ourselves must be diligent in maintaining our faith in a powerful yet loving and merciful God.

The following story I got off the computer, and it is one of the best explanations of the nature of God I have ever seen. A man went into a barbershop to have his hair cut and his beard trimmed. As the barber began to work, they began to have a good conversation. They talked about many things and various subjects. When they eventually touched on the subject of God, the barber said that he didn't believe God exists. The customer asked why he said that. The barber answered that you just have to go out in the street to realize God does not exist. If God exists, there would not be so many sick people or abandoned children. If God existed, there would be no suffering or pain. A loving God would not allow such things. The customer thought for a moment but didn't respond because he didn't want to start an argument. The barber finished his job, and the customer left the shop.

Just after he left the shop, he saw a man in the street with long, stringy, dirty hair and an untrimmed beard. The customer went back into the shop and said to the barber that barbers do not exist. The barber was surprised and replied that he was a barber and he had just cut the customer's hair. No, he answered, because if they existed, there would be no people with dirty long hair and untrimmed beards like the man outside. But the barber exclaimed, "We do exist, and that's what happens when people do not come to the barbershop." The customer agreed and said that God too does exist. But some people do not go to Him and do not look to Him for help. That's why there's so much pain and suffering in the world.

Only God can make anyone rest secure, and only God can guarantee that you will always be taken care of. But we have to interact with Him on a daily basis and do what He wants. No one else is like Him. No one else answers prayer.

CHAPTER 2

Our Eternal Destiny

He who sows to the Spirit will of the Spirit reap
everlasting life.—Galatians 6:8

To fall in love with God is the greatest romance;
to seek Him is the greatest adventure; to find Him
is the greatest human achievement.—Anonymous

EVERYONE KNOWS JOHN 3:16 says, "God so
loved the world that He gave His only begotten Son
that whoever believes in Him should not perish but have
everlasting life." In other words, we humans will endure
spiritually even beyond what we know as civilization here
on this earth. Science tells us that the sun in our solar
system generates light and heat to supply us with energy.
This energy is from atomic explosions that consume the
hydrogen that makes up about 75 percent of the sun. Thus
our sun is continuously degenerating and cannot last forever.
Fortunately this is a long process, and science predicts our
solar system will go on for about five billion years. But we
humans will endure even after our solar system is gone!

But how is it that God has planned to spend a joyful eternity with human beings who have led good lives, while those who have not led such good lives will suffer eternally? How can a God of love and mercy allow this? How can He be happy when so many of His creatures are suffering eternally?

Each religion has its own version of heaven and hell. Generally, people think heaven is a place of eternal joy for those who have lived good lives and hell is a place of punishment for those who have done evil and have not repented. Matthew 28:30 says, "I am with you always even to the end of the world." So "He has appointed a day on which He will judge the world in righteousness" (Acts 17:31). "Satan and all his cohorts will be thrown into a pool of fire and sulfur and will be tormented forever" (Revelation 20:7–9).

However, there is another factor in Christian theology. "Purgatory is an intermediate state after physical death in which those destined for Heaven can undergo purification so as to achieve the holiness necessary to enter into the joy of Heaven" (from Wikipedia). Purgatory is associated with the Latin Rite of the Catholic Church, the Anglicans of the Anglo-Catholic tradition, and High Church Lutheranism. Also Eastern Orthodox churches pray for the dead and hope for a general reprieve. Furthermore, some Jews believe in after-death purification, and purgatory is part of the Jewish concept of Gehenna.

So there is another chance for us even if we die in sin. God in His great mercy allows for some people to be saved from purgatory, where they suffer for their sins but are given time for purification through prayers offered in heaven and on earth. Furthermore there is an indication that the state we live in after death allows some rational, purposeful function. Evidence from life-after-death experiences indicates humans can have rational thoughts after death of the body. (See George C. Richie, MD. *Ordered to Return: My Life after Dying.* Charlottesville, Virginia: Hampton Road Publishing, 1998.) Some people may be able to repent and accept God's forgiveness while in purgatory.

Seems to me that a God of mercy and great love would allow forgiveness in this process of purgatory. Otherwise, how could He be so ecstatically happy for all eternity knowing that many of the beloved people He created are in so much agony? If, however, He provides purgatory as an escape mechanism and they still choose not to repent even after experiencing the intense fire, then the blame is on them and not God. Using their free will, they can still choose not to enter God's eternal peace. Hell may exist, but there may be very few people there.

CHAPTER 3

God in Early Development of Human Civilization

God cannot give us happiness and peace apart from Himself, because it is not there. There is no such thing.—C. S. Lewis

Holiness is not the way to Christ. Christ is the way to holiness.—Anonymous

IF THERE IS a God who created this universe for His purposes, then we should see His hand in development of human civilization. It is thought that several different civilizations formed more or less simultaneously and independently in different parts of the world. The oldest major community was established in Mesopotamia about 10,000 BC. Other settlements occurred, for example in Peru and along the Yangtze River in China. Somehow people agreed to live together in these communities.

Some think that earlier societies may have been formed naturally by men. People may have lived in nonstate societies, in small bands or chiefdoms where everybody was equal, or in ones where paternalistic authority reigned. They may have lived civilly by natural instincts. Seems to me, however, that there must have been some pious individuals who had some concept of God who could show these people how to behave and how to interact appropriately with one another.

When communities formed, men invented the wheel and planted the first cereal crops. They formulated a cursive script and established mathematical as well as astronomical and agricultural principles. Men are very clever, but it's hard to imagine how these primitive people organized themselves to live together peacefully on their own in these early settlements.

The patriarch Abraham (1813 BC) in the book of Genesis in the Bible had a strong belief in God and passed on his faith to his family members. He had no Bible to read, no church to go to, or no pastor to talk to, yet he deeply believed. Abraham's grandson, Jacob, had twelve sons who each had large families. Abraham passed on his faith to his offspring, which became the nation of Israel and still exists 3,500 years later.

Abraham lived almost two thousand years before Christ. What about those eight thousand preceding years when early communities were developing? Was anyone around then to guide people in godly ways? The Bible mentions Melchizedek in Psalm 110 and says he was a prototype of the Messiah. Genesis 14:18 says he was a priest of the Most High God.

JOSEPH BOROWITZ

Could there have been godly human beings in the order of Melchizedek during the eight thousand years of development of communities in this world of ours?

In the time of Abraham, the tribes around him waged war against some local kings and in the process carried off Abraham's nephew, Lot and his possessions. Abraham organized 318 men born of his own household and pursued the invaders and brought back Lot and all his goods and his people as well. I assume this was done as peacefully as possible. Then Abraham was visited by Melchizedek, king of Salem, who said, "Blessed be God the most high who has delivered your enemies into your hands" (Hebrews 13–16). He was a godly influence in Abraham's life. So this Christlike figure came to Abraham and shared some godly words. Could this have occurred regularly during the previous eight thousand years?

God also guided society through the Old Testament prophets. These people were called by God and were filled with the Holy Spirit. They spoke God's Word to people who needed help. Moses, for example, was called to rescue the Hebrew people from slavery in Egypt and then to lead them into the land God had promised them. We mentioned previously (Psalm 78) how people had problems relating to God. It was Moses again and again who had to bring the people back to a right relationship with God.

Sometimes, due to bad kings, the Israelites turned away from God. Concern for the poor, the widow, and the stranger was replaced by oppression. Bribes, extortion, and dishonest gain became commonplace. Prophets like Deborah, Samuel, Elijah, Elisha, and others were filled with God's Spirit to speak the Word of God to people who had drifted away.

Jonah was a prophet called by God to speak to the people of Nineveh, the Assyrian capital. Jonah did not want to help Israel's enemy, but finally, he did so. Later, the Assyrians conquered Israel and took many of the Israelites into captivity. So Jonah may have helped his own people by having a good influence on Nineveh before the captivity.

The small southern kingdom of Judah alternated between worship of foreign gods and worship of the true God. Good kings pulled the people back from idol worship, but bad kings reversed that. Obediah and Joel were prophets who worked to correct the work of bad kings. Nahum and Jeremiah also lived in Jerusalem at the time. Thus many prophets were important messengers from God sent to guide His people in the early years of Judaism.

Athens, Greece, was a center of learning in the time before Christ. Socrates was renowned for his Socratic method, which was an approach to discriminate between truth and error by asking questions. He claimed to "know nothing" and said of his Socratic method that he was like a midwife and posed questions to help people determine underlying truth.

Plato, a student of Socrates, founded the Academy, which was the first institution of higher learning in the Western world. Aristotle, a student of Plato, believed that created things have meaning in themselves and truth can be obtained by observation. Aristotle is the patron saint of modern science. Plato, however, distrusted the senses and was like many who believe that nothing in creation can be fully understood apart from the Creator.

So the Greek philosophers Socrates (470 BC), Plato (~425 BC) and Aristotle (384 BC) had strong ideas about God. Socrates emphasized the importance of love in people's lives and foreshadowed Christ who also said "Love one another" (John 15:2). Socrates believed that God arranges everything for a purpose. Plato said, "Knowledge is not entirely empirical but comes also from divine insight." Furthermore he believed in the immortality of the soul. Aristotle was more practical and more scientific than either Plato or Socrates. He thought that men could get a complete understanding of creation by making careful observations using their own sensory abilities. The debate over the absolute need for God in human understanding continues today.

Thus in the years of the development of civilization, people like Melchizedek, Socrates, and the prophets were around to bring a godly influence into the affairs of men.

In ancient Rome (about 300 BC), the pontifex maximus was a high priest and leader of a small body of pontifexes.

The name means "bridge builder," and the pontifexes were the ones who smoothed the bridge between gods and men. Like the Greeks, the Romans had strong ideas about God, and there was a need for godly men in that society before the coming of Christ. These men carried out religious duties and rituals previously performed by the king in the Roman Empire. They had religious and also some political functions. They operated mostly in the first three centuries before Christ. Julius Caesar became a pontifex in 73 BC and was promoted to pontifex maximus in 63 BC. The title survives from the time of Pope Leo I (AD 440–461) who took the title pontifex maximus, and the name has been adopted by all subsequent popes. The word *pope* predates the title *pontifex* and is the Greek word for "father" used by children.

As C. S. Lewis says, there is no real peace in human lives without a healthy appreciation of God. Societies that formed on earth before the time of Christ were aware of the need for a strong theological orientation in order for humans to have a peaceful existence.

CHAPTER 4

Church and State

With humility comes wisdom.—Proverbs 11:2

Let us meditate on the gospels. Amidst the confusion of so many human words, the gospel is the only voice that enlightens and attracts, that consoles and quenches thirst.—Pope John XXIII

BOTH STRONG SPIRITUALITY and good government are necessary for a healthy society. However, the relationship between the church and the state down through the centuries has not always been good. A really bad example of church-and-state interactions was France before the revolution. But let's start with a good example: the early years of the United States of America.

In forming the American government, the patriots had a dream of religious freedom, and they also tried to balance the executive, legislative, and judicial branches of government so as to maintain this ideal. They followed the advice of Charles Louis Montesquieu, who wrote a book, *The Spirit of the Laws*, in 1748. He emphasized the need for balanced forces pushing against each other to prevent tyranny.

The First Amendment of the Constitution of the United States forbids interference of religion and politics with one another. However there is still a close relationship between faith and loyalty to the USA. "In God we trust" is printed on our money. On the back of the one dollar bill, we see "Novus ordo seclorum," meaning "A new order of the ages." This is a reference to the new American era, a new and better form of government. We swear on a Bible to tell the truth in courts of law. The newly elected president of the USA raises his right hand and puts his left hand on a Bible when he takes his oath of office and swears to uphold the Constitution. Also the First Amendment provides for freedom of religion and guarantees equal voice to people of different faiths.

The American government is not a democracy but a republic since senators, state representatives, and the president are elected by the people and are expected to represent the voters who elected them. The president has veto power over Congress. Supreme Court members are appointed by the president and are not elected officials. Supreme Court pronouncements on abortion and same-sex marriage go against godly principles. This needs to be corrected. Our laws must be righteous and not just the whims of public opinion or the opinions of a few lawyers.

The Constitution of the United States, including the first ten amendments (which is the Bill of Rights), safeguards citizens of the USA, giving specific guarantees of personal freedom and rights with clear limits to government power. The Declaration of Independence gives three examples of inalienable rights given to all human beings by their Creator: life, liberty, and the pursuit of happiness. Governments should protect these rights. Abraham Lincoln argued that the Declaration of Independence is a statement of principles by which the United States Constitution should be interpreted.

We have problems now as our American government has evolved with a progressive movement. Presidents Teddy Roosevelt, Woodrow Wilson, and Franklin Roosevelt thought that the Constitution was too restrictive and needed to be modified to deal with conditions that did not exist at the time of our Founding Fathers. They didn't think God's laws involving life, liberty, and the pursuit of happiness were enough and that men could do better. They thought that government could do it by themselves. Hence the New Deal program to eliminate poverty and establish Social Security. This Progressive movement has changed our government into a complex of agencies that are established by Congress to work on different tasks like clean air or clean water. Then "experts" are hired by the government to accomplish these tasks. If something goes wrong or doesn't work out as intended, the agencies themselves decide what to do. They are their own bosses and their own judges. There is a mass of confusion and lack of clear authority lines, so we've lost our "balance of power" considered so important by the Founding Fathers. What are we going to do to reestablish a good simple governmental system with balance of power?

People in important administrative positions in American government must be humble and realize that they have the natural human tendency to be selfish and not put God first. You've all heard the motto of the USA, "E pluribus unum," meaning "One out of many." Some say we have too much pluribus and not enough unum. We are in desperate need for people like Abraham Lincoln who can take personal responsibility and guide our agencies with godly wisdom. Maybe heads of agencies should be elected by the people every two years?

Numerous departments and agencies are part of our US government. Cabinet posts headed by secretaries directly assist the president. There are now about fifteen such units, including Agriculture, Commerce, Defense, Labor, Homeland Security, etc. Secretaries are nominated by the president and approved by the Senate.

Dr. Larry Arnn, president of Hillsdale College in Michigan, recently commented on the Department of Education. He has good insight into the operations of this department even though Hillsdale is a private college and receives no federal funding. He says that the Department of Education spends an enormous amount of money, about 7 percent of the federal budget. This explains part of the huge debt of about $20 trillion, which our nation carries and which will be a burden to our descendants.

President Trump mentioned that he was thinking of abolishing the Department of Education. Dr. Arnn was pleased with this since the program is poorly handled. The money is given to states "on condition." The conditions are "myriad, confusing and usually ugly when they are understood."

Dr. Arnn says that "Title IV of the Higher Education Act governs Federal student aid and numbers 500 pages." A lawyer advised Dr. Arnn not to read it. The lawyer himself tried to read it and did not understand it. The lawyer also mentioned that the only person in his law firm who has any understanding of this five-hundred-page document is a specialist in the firm who has devoted considerable time studying it.

The hope of Dr. Arnn is that Trump leads us back to conservative ideals of our Founding Fathers. We need to recover the godly values of the Declaration of Independence. Dr. Arnn believes that the Constitution of the United States can also be revived to reform our government based on godly principles agreed upon by people who love one another. Then we can pursue things of mutual benefit.

President Trump will have a difficult time doing this because the authority of these two documents is in decline.

Most scholars reject them as obsolete and some consider them evil. Still Dr. Arnn hopes Trump will be able to correct our government, which has swollen out of control and is centralized to an extent not imagined in the Constitution. It seems every aspect of our society has regulations. "Every employer, every school, many clubs, and even family life itself are subject to rules too complex for the layperson to grasp." Trump would "drain the swamp" and abolish the Department of Education as well as the Environmental Protection Agency.

Now let's mention really bad church-and-state relationships. The Holy Roman Empire was a multiethnic complex of territories that began in the year AD 800 when Charlemagne was crowned emperor by Pope Leo III. He and the Carolingian family reigned till 888. Government was an elective monarchy. High-ranking noblemen usually elected one of their peers. The power of the emperor was limited. Lords and vassals were given autonomy in their own territories. After a series of civil wars, Otto I was crowned emperor in the year 962. There was no official capital, but there was a close association between fourteen nations including Germany, Italy, France, Switzerland, Poland, and the Czech Republic. Emperors employed bishops in administrative affairs, and often, the emperor would determine who would be appointed to ecclesiastical offices. Pope Gregory VII objected to Emperor Henry IV's interference in church affairs. Henry

IV then persuaded his bishops to excommunicate the pope! The pope in turn excommunicated Henry IV in the year 1076. Henry then repented and received a lifting of the excommunication. However, the conflict continued. Gregory again excommunicated Henry, and Henry had Clement III installed as pope. This illustrates the awkward power struggles that characterized the interactions between the church and the state in the Holy Roman Empire. Somehow the empire continued on for some time, but it was dissolved in the year 1806 when Napoleon defeated Francis II at Austerlitz. Voltaire, the French philosopher, commented that "The Holy Roman Empire was in no way holy, nor Roman nor an Empire."

The French Revolution (1789–1799) ended the monarchy and replaced it with a republic. Both King Louis XVI and Queen Marie Antoinette were executed in 1793. During the Reign of Terror (1793–1794), twenty thousand people were killed—many of them priests. Many other priests were expelled from the country. The people associated priests with the monarchy. The church owned 10 percent of the property in France and paid a reduced property tax.

After the revolution, French society became secularized and even approved same-sex marriage. Not only was the monarchy ineffective, but the clergy obviously did not have the proper influence on society in the years before the revolution.

Globally, the French Revolution gave rise to an increase in republics, democracies, and other forms of government. Both the Russian revolutions of 1905 and 1917 occurred just a few years after the French Revolution.

If we look back on history, we should be able to evaluate the relative effectiveness of political and ecclesiastical authority in building each individual society. Roman and Greek ideals strongly influenced Western views on the subject. The Western Roman Empire existed from 285 BC to AD 476. Rome was its capital, and in the year AD 100, it had a population of over a million and was the largest city in the world. The Eastern Roman Empire was centered in Constantinople and functioned from 330 BC to AD 1453. The Christian Eastern Orthodox Church was strong in the Eastern Roman Empire.

The Western Roman Empire existed for some three hundred years before Christ came. There was relative peace in the world from 27 BC to AD 180 (Pax Romana). Some say it was an ideal time to initiate Christianity. The Romans had built an extensive system of roads that made it easier for the apostles and disciples to spread the Good News. God timed it well. The world needed to hear the message. Did it immediately change the world? No, but it got us off to a good start, and we're much better off since Christ came. Most importantly, many people experienced "peace which the world cannot give." With the adoption of Christianity as the state religion in the year AD 313, the Western Roman emperor Constantine began to issue decrees on both religious matters and government, so these areas were somewhat coordinated at that time.

People today are still too busy to give much priority to spiritual things. Most likely it was the same in ancient times. That real deep-down peace is not accessible except with God. The world has always had many distractions. But now we have the full story, and with the Bible, we all have the full opportunity to live deeply spiritual lives.

The combination of religious and political authority has a long history on earth, and their coexistence supports the idea that both are needed in human society. In the year 680 BC, city-states in ancient Greece had magistrates or archons who had some power in both areas. The archon was responsible for some civic religious activities and for supervision of some major trials in the courts.

Probably the most regimented societies in the world are the Islamic states, which combine both religious and political authority. Islam was founded by Mohammed who was born in Mecca, Saudi Arabia, in AD 572. As a young man, he married a wealthy widow and had much leisure time for religious contemplation. Judaism and Christianity had been around for several hundred years, but the people of that area worshiped many idols.

Mohammed went annually to Mount Hira to meditate and pray. One year, he came back to Mecca and declared that he had a vision in a cave on Mount Hira and that Allah had chosen him to be a prophet. He preached this message for several years and gained a number of followers. This caused friction with other established beliefs. When people threatened to kill him, Mohammed left Mecca and fled to Medina in AD 622. He then reorganized his followers and returned to Mecca in AD 630 and took control of the city. He was acknowledged as a prophet of Islam by all of Arabia.

Islam is not only a religion but a complete theocratic-political and spiritual governance of mankind. So Islamic states are unique in combining spiritual, political, and social authority.

When Mohammed died at age 60, his followers collected what had been said and written about him (he himself couldn't read or write) and created the Qu'ran (Koran in English), which is the holy book of the Islamic people.

Mohammed's death left the Muslims confused because he did not give them directions about who was to be his successor. Amidst much debate, they elected Abu Bakr, an early convert and trusted companion of Mohammed. He took the title of caliph. The caliphate came to embody the religious and political leadership of the community.

Also after Mohammed's death, a minority group in Medina believed that Ali b Abi Talib, first cousin and son-in-law of Mohammed (married to Mohammed's daughter, Fatima) was better qualified than Abu Bakr and formed Shi'at Ali ("party of Ali"). The Shi'a was against the election of a successor and believed their candidate, as a descendent of Mohammed, was a more appropriate leader. The caliphs, however, are considered to be orthodox maintainers of all the regulations of Islam and became known as Sunni Islam. Several other subdivisions also exist. The Sufi orders are more mystical Islamists, and the Shiks of India combine Islamic and Hindu beliefs and practices.

In the years after Mohammed, most of the desert-dwelling Bedouin tribes of Arabia pledged allegiance to the Prophet of Islam, and they spread Islam to the surrounding areas. After the death of Mohammed in AD 632, the Islamic Caliphate extended from the Atlantic Ocean in the west to Central Asia. People need good governance in both political and in religious affairs. Thus nearly every nation on earth has had both political and some sort of ecclesiastical structure in its makeup.

The Holy Roman Empire folded in 1806 but has emerged again in the form of the European Union (EU). It has twenty-eight member nations, with Germany being the largest. There are about five hundred million people in the EU. It has no single capital, but the most important offices are in Brussels, Belgium. The EU provides for free movement of people, goods, and services in its territory. Nineteen of the member states use the euro currency. The EU generates about 24 percent of the gross domestic product of the world.

The flag of the EU has a circle of twelve stars on a blue background. The twelve stars indicate completeness. No matter how many nations join the EU, the flag will remain the same. The twelve stars represent the "corona stellarum duodecim" of the "woman of the Apocalypse" in chapter 12 of the book of Revelation in the Bible.

The EU government is complex. Like the USA, they have two legislative bodies The Parliament is elected by citizens according to population and has a total of 751 members who serve a five-year term. The Council of Ministers is the other legislative body composed of twenty-eight ministers appointed by the governments of each state. There are ten different configurations of ministers depending on the nature of the legislation. If the topic is agriculture, then experts in agriculture are involved. The presidency of the Council of Ministers rotates among the member states every six months. The Parliament and Council of Ministers coordinate with each other in enacting legislation.

The European Commission is the executive arm of the EU. It is composed of appointed representatives from each of the twenty-eight states. The president of the commission serves for two years and is nominated by the European Council and approved by Parliament. The European Commission has primary responsibility for the operation of the government.

The European Council is a group of the heads of state or of government of each of the twenty-eight EU members. They meet four times a year. The president of this body is elected by the group itself. The president of the European Commission is also a member of the European Council.

JOSEPH BOROWITZ

The EU is 48 percent Catholic, 12 percent Protestant, 8 percent Orthodox, 16 percent atheist/agnostic, and 2 percent Muslim. There is no official representation or provision made for religion in the EU government.

Rights and liberties exist only in separate and independent nations. The EU is not a constitutional government. It is an administrative state ruled by bureaucrats. It attempts to do away with rights and liberty and replaces them with welfare and regulations. Constitutional government succeeds only in the nation state where just powers are derived from consent of the governed (E. Euler, speech at Hillsdale College, 2016).

Where there is disrespect for human life in any of its forms, societies degenerate. In Nazi Germany even before the Holocaust, handicapped young people were euthanized. They were precious to their families but were deemed useless to society and were eliminated. Likewise, older people who were not capable of productive work were done away with. A superior society with strong Arian traits and no imperfections was sought after. However, all life is honorable and lovable. Governments should be aware of this and not judge, but should respect life in all its forms and circumstances. One weakness in the EU is the lack of mention of either religious principles or respect for human life in any of its documents. Apparently these were considered domains of individual member states and were not dealt with at the Union level. The recent resignation of Great Britain from the EU may reflect the lack of a strong spiritual basis for the Union. Time will tell whether the EU can prosper without secure agreement on religious principles.

During the dark days of the Civil War in the USA, Abraham Lincoln in one of his proclamations said, "It is the duty of nations as well as of men to own their dependence upon the overruling power of God; to confess their sins and transgressions in humble sorrow, yet with assured hope that genuine repentance will lead to mercy and pardon; and to recognize the sublime truth announced in the Holy Scriptures and proven by all history, that those nations only are blessed whose God is the Lord. We in the USA have been recipients of the choicest bounties of heaven. We have been preserved, these many years, in peace and prosperity. We have grown in numbers, wealth, and power as no other nation has ever grown, but we have forgotten God. It behooves us, then to humble ourselves before the offended power, to confess our national sins, and to pray for clemency and forgiveness." Now, even more than in Lincoln's day, we have a need to humble ourselves before God, confess our sins, and ask for forgiveness.

"Man shall not live by bread alone but by every word that proceeds from the mouth of God" (Matthew 4:4).

CHAPTER 5

Examples of How a Deep Experience with God Can Change Lives

A man's grasp should exceed his reach, or what's heaven for?—Robert Browning

THE MOST FAMOUS conversion experience was that of Saint Paul. He was a grouchy pharisee nobody loved. He enjoyed arresting and punishing Christians for their faith. On his way to Damascus, he was blinded and fell to the ground. God had to deal with him powerfully in a physical way to get his attention. Saul was mystified. He thought he was leading a productive life and serving God. He was told he was not doing the right thing. "You're kicking against the goads" (Acts 26:14). Saul was not working according to God's plan. Saul asked, "Who are you?" He said, "I am Jesus whom you are persecuting" (Acts 26:15). Jesus said, "I am sending you to the Gentiles that they may turn from darkness to light and from the power of Satan to God." Later Ananias prayed for him, and he received his sight and his name was changed to Paul. The wisdom of all the letters he wrote is tremendous, and he has enriched us all with his insight and great love.

Some believe the word *Bible* is an acronym for "basic instructions before leaving earth." As such, it provides the fundamentals for living a good life. But the Bible continues to be written in each of our lives. So stories of incredible things that happen to each of us are to be shared and are meant to encourage all of us in our earthly journey.

An American soldier in Vietnam was shot in the left thigh by small arms fire. Then a grenade exploded near him and fractured some bones in his left foot. That ended the war for him. They sent him back to the States. His doctor asked him what he did before he was drafted. He said he was a rookie running back for the Pittsburgh Steelers. (You may have heard of him; his name is Rocky Bleier.) The doctor replied that he'd have to find something else to do because the US Army classified him as 40 percent disabled.

But when Rocky was wounded, he made a vow to God on the battlefield to become the best person he could be. He still thought he could be a good running back. So he started a training program for himself four months after the injuries. It was very difficult, but he did his best. In the Steeler training camp, he came out last in the forty-yard dash—even behind the big offensive linemen. Then a hamstring injury delayed his recovery another year. He talked to a priest friend who was his advisor in high school and when Rocky played for Notre Dame. The priest said that he should be sure that it is not his decision alone but God's also. A wise counselor can serve as a spiritual support similar to a small prayer group.

Rocky still believed he could do well as a running back and that it was God's will, so he persisted. He had to play on special teams for a while but finally made the starting lineup, mainly as a blocking back. But he also contributed to the team with his running and pass catching. He thanked God for the opportunities he was given, especially when he was able to help the Steelers win the Super Bowl against the Vikings.

Another powerful true story involved a lady who was an undertaker's wife. She helped out at the funeral home in greeting people and helping to select caskets. Her daughters entertained themselves by playing jump rope with the pew cords and hide-and-seek among the caskets. They were a happy family, but her husband died suddenly and left her empty. She was aware of the great emptiness within. She knew that the large vacuum within would not go away quickly; it would need time. So she did not try to fill the emptiness right away by getting remarried. She entered school and studied to become a licensed undertaker herself. The lady and her two daughters matured greatly in the aftermath of the father's death. They did the right thing. People who knew the family complimented them on handling the situation so well. They thought it was because the family was in the funeral business and were used to death and dying. The lady denied it and said that it was only by reliance on the mercy and strength of Jesus Christ that they were able to endure. A deeply spiritual small prayer group would have been a blessing to her and her daughters in their time of trial.

A young man in a tough neighborhood in Stockton, California, got into drugs in high school and actually became a drug dealer in his area. Another boy who owed him some money asked to see him and brought a friend with him. Earl Smith thought that these people simply wanted to pay what was owed. However, the boy actually brought his friend with him to do away with Earl. His friend had a gun and shot Earl six times. He was taken to the ER in serious condition. He was deathly afraid, as you can imagine, lying there waiting for treatment. However, he had a deep spiritual experience and was told not to worry but to change his life and that he would become a chaplain at the notorious prison San Quentin on San Francisco Bay. He recovered from his injuries and decided to go to Bible college and enter into the ministry. He also married a fine woman who encouraged him to give up drugs and become a preacher. He graduated from Bible college and worked for the Boy Scouts for a while. He applied for the chaplaincy at San Quentin and became the youngest chaplain ever at that prison. During the normal six months' probation period for chaplains at the prison, Earl felt he had not done much and might lose his job.

JOSEPH BOROWITZ

It was Christmas time when Earl discovered the man who shot him was incarcerated at San Quentin. He thought he had forgiven him, but when he saw him face-to-face, thoughts of hatred came back. All sorts of vengeful thoughts came to mind when he met him. However, he managed to say, "Thank you for shooting me. God used you to get to me." He gave the man a box of Christmas cards and had to leave abruptly. He was overcome with emotion and went back to his office and sobbed. He didn't realize he had been carrying so much pain, and then he saw that the lack of forgiveness had caused him to hurt others. Afterward, he was grateful and thanked God for the cleansing experience. He devised new ways of dealing with the inmates.

So many stabbings and murders occurred at San Quentin that it was considered one of the most dangerous places on earth. Earl made a deal with the inmates so that if there were no stabbings or killings in the prison for a couple of months, the inmates would have a special dinner and each could invite one guest. The inmates made good on the deal, and the banquet was a great success.

Earl Smith wanted to know how these men kept their dreams alive in such a hopeless place as San Quentin. He arranged to play chess with them. The intense concentration needed in the game lowered their defenses, and they would share intimate things with him. One inmate who was a convicted murderer confessed he had a bad relationship with his father. He and Earl became close so that Earl felt that he had left a piece of himself in the gas chamber when the man was executed. This inmate told him that he would put in a good word for Earl in heaven. In this unusual way, Earl was able to connect with the people he was trying to help.

Earl Smith also started a choir at the prison and reestablished the baseball team. He recently retired after twenty-three years as chaplain at San Quentin. What a miraculous change occurred when a teenage addict and drug dealer became an effective chaplain and counselor in a notorious prison!

Late one Christmas Eve, a lady was waiting up for her only son. He came home from his first semester at college and got a job at the mall. Her husband was a mail carrier and had gone to bed early since he had been working overtime in the busy Christmas season. About 11:00 p.m., the phone rang. Her son always called when he was running late. However, it was not her son but a nurse in the emergency room at the hospital. There had been an accident, and her son had serious head and neck injuries. She woke her husband, and they went to the hospital. Their son was transferred to another hospital that had a neurosurgeon, so they drove there also. The lady was overwhelmed with grief and begged God for mercy. Nevertheless, her son died. She and her husband drove home in the early hours of Christmas morning. The house was decorated with bright lights and holiday trimmings, but the lady was so upset that she had to brace herself on the furniture to even stand up.

The driver of the other car was drunk and escaped with only minor injuries. He had swerved over into the other lane and collided with the lady's son's car. His blood alcohol was far beyond the safe limit. In the time before the trial took place, the lady was beside herself with a morbid desire for justice to be done. She could think of nothing else. She gave up all her social activities except for going to church. She struggled with things she had heard at church about forgiving those that hurt you.

Finally, the trial took place, and both the lady and her husband attended. The charge was murder, but the sentence handed down was only for ten years' probation. The man who had killed her son was not imprisoned, and furthermore, his driver's license was not revoked. It seemed so unfair and unjust. However the probation required the man to spend one night in jail on the weekends and to speak at meetings of MADD (Mothers Against Drunk Drivers).

The lady went to one of the MADD meetings only because it took place at her son's high school and there was a memorial for him there that same night. When she saw the man who killed her son, the lady walked out of the room. However, she had the courage to come back and heard him admit that he had killed a man while driving drunk, and he confessed to be very sorry about the whole thing.

Could it be that she had misjudged this man and that he simply was an individual with great personal problems? She lived in a neighborhood close to his and noticed one day that he was walking along the street, and she stopped to talk to him. She detected alcohol on his breath. She said, "You don't need a driver's license in the condition you're in." He tried to give her his driver's license, and she asked him how often he drank. He said, "Every day till I go to bed."

So one weekend, he showed up at jail and they found high blood alcohol, and he was imprisoned to serve his ten-year sentence. She visited him in jail and asked him if he would like to join her and her husband in a Bible study. They arranged to pick him up one day a week and have dinner at their house and do a Bible study in the evening before they took him back to jail.

Eventually she asked him to forgive her for hating him. So forming a small Bible study group helped this lady to do the right thing and live a productive life. God wants us not only to forgive our enemies but do good for them also.

At her husband's suggestion, the lady started inviting friends over for dinner. The man who killed her son would help by mowing the lawn. She was able to forgive, and it brought healing into her life. When we live by God's rules, then life has a good purpose, and we can overcome even gigantic problems and enjoy the fullness that God promised us.

Most people believe that the Bible gives God's advice on how humans should conduct their lives. However, men have their own opinions, such as the Supreme Court in approving abortion and permitting same-sex marriage. We, like Peter and the other apostles, should agree that we will obey God rather than men.

CHAPTER 6

Nature of Dialogue
Between Human Beings

Earth produces nothing worse than an ungrateful
man.—Ausonius

BASICALLY, HUMANS ARE social creatures. We crave positive interactions with others. So relationships are very important to each one of us. Physicians understand that positive interactions between human beings are critical for our health. Imagine that! Your very life depends on the quality of your casual as well as close friendships.

International relationships also depend on good dialogue between people. Diplomats must be adept at maintaining peace with other people and the countries they represent. So world peace depends on people who can communicate effectively and prevent any negative feelings between populations.

Eric Berne wrote a book in 1964 entitled *Games People Play*. He says we all have inferior feelings that stem from childhood when we were weaker, smaller, and less knowledgeable than most other people. Sometimes when we interact with other people, we try to correct this inferior position. If we talk about cars, ours is the best. It gets better gas mileage, doesn't show the dirt, has faster acceleration, etc., than yours. If we talk about houses, ours is the best. It is built better, easier to maintain, on a street with less traffic than yours. So the beat goes on no matter what the topic.

The basic unit of communication between people is called a transaction. It can arise from any one of the three basic personalities within our nature: Parent, Adult, or Child.

The Parent and the Child are essentially completely formed by the age of five. Mostly, our Parent is a copy of our own parents' personalities. The Parent is not always logical and can be simply a series of dos and don'ts. Do clean your plate. Don't waste food. Don't play in the street. Look both ways before crossing the street. Prejudice is usually located in the Parent part of our personalities. The words *always* and *never* are typical of parental conversations. The healthy parental personality has an appreciation of the need to live a balanced life with a sense of responsibility and a respect for legitimate authority.

The Adult begins to develop at ten months of age when locomotion begins and continues to grow throughout life. Our occupations often require good Adult logical thinking. However a good Child is also important for us to survive in society. A healthy Child provides an appreciation of humor and helps us deal effectively with others. The lawyer uses his Child when playing with the dog in the evenings. He may have a good education and a strong Adult, but he still needs the Child part to be a fully rounded personality.

The Child in the personality usually develops naturally in a loving family. An encouraging attitude on the part of the parents helps form the sense of humor and promotes play to nurture healthy Child personality development.

When humans speak to each other, they can employ the Parent, Adult, or Child personalities. These three natures have three distinct attitudes. Transactional analysis involves examining conversations between people to determine the amount of Parent, Adult, or Child (PAC) present in the interaction. An example of a parental transaction between two old ladies waiting on a bus: "Why is the bus always late?" "It never fails. It's a sign of the times." Adult conversations usually have a serious purpose like, "What time is the bus due to arrive?" "It's due at two thirty p.m." An example between two children: "Let's play family. I'll be the mom, and you be the baby." "Why do I always have to be the baby?" Thus the nature of the interaction reflects the individual PAC personality involved.

A crossed transaction occurs when a personality in one person is answered by another personality in another person. For example a mother asks her son, "Is your room tidy yet?" (Parent to Child). The son answers, "I wish you'd stop bugging me" (Child to Child). The boy accuses the mother of being childish and feelings are hurt. Another example, a wife asks the husband, "What's on TV?" (Adult to Adult). The husband says, "Dust" (Parent to Adult). Again feelings are hurt in a crossed transaction.

You may wonder whether there are specific brain areas controlling the Parent, Adult, and Child personalities like the motor cortex, which specifically controls movement of various skeletal muscles. The answer is no, since most of the twelve billion cells of the brain are very much interconnected. Thus emotions, cognition, and behavior are all mixed in together. Electrical stimulation of an area of the brain outside the motor cortex can initiate a complex mixture of results.

When a person has an abnormal PAC construct, they can be a problem in society in general and in prayer groups also. A healthy person, who has a well-developed PAC, can function well in the various situations they find themselves faced with every day. All three parts of our personalities are needed if we are to function well in society.

Passive aggression was first reported by a colonel in the US Army in WW II. He thought it was due to immaturity and to the stress of military service. I first heard of it in officer's training in the US Army Reserve. A psychiatrist described a private second class who worked in the office for him. The soldier showed a habitual pattern of passive resistance to expected work requirements, opposition, and stubbornness.

The doctor described how upset he was with this young man's procrastination, sullenness, and failure to accomplish expected tasks.

A similar problem can be caused by alcohol-addicted or drug-addicted parents. Parents in such a family are at times brutal, doltish, or overindulgent and thus are ineffective. The children are exposed to an environment where they are not safe in expressing anger or frustration. These children have little conscience and have little remorse. None of the parts of the PAC construct function normally. They are said to have a Parent-contaminated Adult and a blocked-out Child.

The child in such a family rejects much of the Parent and replaces it with a modified Adult or Child of his own imagination. He has a desire for self-assertion and is uncompromising and abusive. Such an individual can be devastating if allowed to hold a leadership position in a prayer group or any other type of organization. They do not have the good of the group at heart.

When a child is born late in the family with many older siblings, he is constantly reminded to grow up and to be continuously productive. This person also develops a Parent-contaminated Adult with a blocked-out Child. When he gets a job, he becomes a workaholic and never wants to take a vacation. His family has to force him to take time off. Lack of a sense of humor handicaps this overly serious person the rest of their lives.

Some very serious behavioral abnormalities can occur when the PAC construct is not normal. Manic depression can develop when a child has an alcoholic mother. When the mother is high on alcohol and plays with the child, she is generous with strokes. Then she sometimes loses consciousness when she drinks too much, and the child is alone. When she wakes up, she is sick and pushes the child away. Can you imagine how the child feels with all these drastic changes in behavior? Normally, the Adult is in control and can overcome feelings of depression or mania. But in strong manic depression, the Adult cannot always control the mood swings, and serious depression alternates with extreme mania.

A PAC abnormality leading to criminal tendencies occurs when parents severely beat their children. The child is seriously hurt with deep bruises, and it takes several days for them to recover. Usually this is done with no help or sympathy from the parents. These children realize that the Parent in their family is not good and reject it. Then they form a distorted Parent of their own. They also do not respect grown-ups in general. Thus they have a distorted Parent and Child-contaminated Adult.

John Dillinger, the infamous Depression-era gangster, robbed many banks and killed at least ten men but had no remorse for any of them. His mother died when he was four years old. His father owned a small grocery store and believed in the words of the Bible, "Spare the rod and spoil the child."

So he treated John harshly. John's defective PAC construct included an abnormal Child that generated a desire to do wrong (to rob and kill) and a defective Parent or Adult that failed to stop the unlimited aggression.

Thomas Harris, a colleague of Eric Berne, wrote a book entitled *I'm OK, You're OK* (10 East 53rd Street, New York, New York 10022: Harper and Row Publishers, 1967), which was a sequel to *Games People Play*. Dr. Harris, also a psychiatrist, became world-famous with this best-selling book. The normal interaction between people is "I'm OK, You're OK." However, we know none of us is perfect but that "All have sinned and fallen short of the glory of God" (Romans 3:23). But we accept each other as OK. To maintain this normal position, we should all be eager to engage in stroking or encouraging each other since we all have a "not OK" Child within us. We should also try to build each other up and recognize each other's talents or accomplishments. This satisfies the recognition hunger that is in each of us in this competitive society of ours.

You've all heard that when we get into an argument, we should stop and count to ten before saying anything. This gives the Adult time to function and review the situation and decide to not allow the Parent or Child to take over. This also gives the Adult time to avoid magnifying the problem or jumping to the conclusion "Nobody likes me." This is a good procedure to keep in mind in these pressure situations.

When we do get our feelings hurt, it sometimes involves a "not OK" Child situation. A good, effective prayer at this time is to say, "God, please unhook my 'not OK' Child." We need to console the "not OK" Child and not let it go on without treatment. Remember, what God thinks of you is most important and not what other people think.

Dr. Harris mentions how the "not OK" Child feels when we perform poorly. Our Parent makes it worse by beating on the "not OK" Child. Michael Jordan was an outstanding basketball player for the Chicago Bulls in the 1980s and the 1990s. With Jordan, the Bulls won the NBA championships three years running in 1991–1993. He is said to be the greatest basketball player who ever lived. Yet even he was not perfect. He missed thousands of shots in his career. Obviously, he did not dwell on those shots he missed. It would have been foolish for him to do that. However, we sometimes do that and magnify things. We need to forgive the "not OK" child who performs poorly and keep trying to do our best.

The behavior of Nikita Khrushchev during his talk to the United Nations Assembly at the time of the cold war between the USSR and the rest of the world was discussed by Dr. Harris. Harris mentioned how Khrushchev took off his shoe and banged it on the podium saying "We will bury you." This Parent/Child behavior has no place in international negotiations which must involve largely the Adult with a minimum of the Parent and Child.

In an ideal relationship, like in a good marriage, there is a commitment to "I'm OK, You're OK" and an absence of games being played. Ample stroking and recognition also occurs. Lastly the Adult is open to asking personal, philosophical, and religious questions and deserves an honest Adult reply. These principles apply to international relations as well as in marital situations.

CHAPTER 7

Vitality of Small Prayer Groups

None are so old as those who have outlived their enthusiasm.—Henry David Thoreau

H OW CAN WE come closer to God so that we can be sure of His saving power? Church attendance should help. Yet only 37 percent of the people in the USA go to church (2013 Gallup poll). Abraham Lincoln was a good Christian. He was a holy man of God. I saw his Bible on display in the boarding house across from Ford's Theater. This boarding house where Lincoln was taken after he was shot in the theater is now a museum. Lincoln's Bible was obviously well-worn. Still, he did not go to church. He couldn't find one where people loved one another. What a sad commentary.

So how do we get close to God? One way is to study the Bible. Abraham Lincoln said the Bible is God's greatest gift to mankind. But without a deep belief in God, you can't really understand the Bible. Just to give a simple example, in Romans 12:12, Saint Paul says, "Be joyful in hope, patient in tribulation, and constant in prayer." How can you be joyful in hope in this world with so many problems? You first have to believe deeply in God and be able to place your hope in this God who is powerful and who you know can help you. Saint Paul also said, "Be patient in tribulation." You need to be able to trust in this God who you know can get you through tough situations. You know you can't do it yourself. Lastly, Saint Paul says be constant in prayer. I mentioned this verse to a graduate student at Purdue. He said, "I can't do that. I have to do my experiments carefully and devote all my attention to them so they are absolutely correct. These data are going to be published. I can't be distracted by prayer." I didn't know exactly what to say to this graduate student. But I should have said that somehow we need to do our work and at the same time ask for God's help. I know I can't do the things I need to do without His help. So Saint Paul is right—we need to pray constantly. Only with a deep belief in the validity of the Bible can we understand what the Bible says, and only then can we really be effective in our life's work.

I was brought up in the Catholic Church and went to a Catholic grade school and a Catholic high school. However the deep significance of the whole of Christianity passed me by. At the age of forty-five, I was a full professor at Purdue, married to a fine lady, and had two really good sons, but I did not go to church regularly and wasn't happy. Another faculty member at Purdue suggested I go to a Full Gospel Businessmen's Fellowship International (FGBFI) meeting in

October 1978. The speaker that night was very persuasive, and after his talk, I went up for baptism in the Holy Spirit. It was a deep experience for me, and it changed my life. The Holy Spirit is a real power of the Blessed Trinity. Without Him and a deep faith in God, there is no possibility of miracles.

The FGBFI is a charismatic, international, nondenominational Christian sect with greeters to make everyone feel welcome, lively music, and powerful sermons. They are a parachurch group and usually meet in motels once a month on Saturday night. It's called Full Gospel because they believe that the whole of the Bible is true and God's power has no limit.

The great enthusiasm at Full Gospel meetings is impressive and is, no doubt, what Christ had in mind when He came to earth. My two teenage sons and I attended FGBFI for five years, and it was a great joy. I still can have good Christian fellowship with them thirty-five years later. They understand the Christian message.

As a result of my baptism in the Holy Spirit, I've been going to small prayer groups for thirty-six years and have attended about 3,600 small group meetings. It has been a fantastic experience. Psalm 16:3 says, "How excellent are the Lord's faithful people. My greatest pleasure is to be with them." That statement is true! These charismatic meetings have been my greatest pleasure. They are charismatic, emphasizing the Holy Spirit, but everyone is welcome and no one is excluded.

Some groups don't know when to quit, so we limit our time together. Our meetings last only one hour. We meet in the chapel at church and start by singing traditional hymns with some charismatic songs, like "Oh the Holy Ghost Will Set Your Feet A-dancing." The singing brings us together and is a great joy. One distinguished long-time charismatic lady in her late eighties got up and began to dance in the aisles when we sang the Holy Ghost song. Our singing lasts for about twenty-five minutes, and everyone participates whether they have a good voice or not.

This is followed by a meditation or a story, maybe from *Guideposts* or some other inspirational sources. We try to have something powerful every week; something that will cut deep into our hard hearts and bring us closer to God. We finish up with a discussion of the meditation or with some rote prayers.

Charismatic hugs at the beginning and at the end are vital parts of our meetings. They make us all feel welcome and loved and wanted.

These small groups can add a lot of zest to your life. Abraham Lincoln would have enjoyed being a part of one of these groups. Everyone in our group at church looks forward to Friday nights. When people are dedicated and all come together with open hearts to allow the Holy Spirit to work, it is a great joy. Many churches already have small prayer groups but more are needed. It's good also to have them at work where people can meet maybe over the lunch period. Just a few people meeting together for godly discussions can have a great beneficial effect on an organization.

In defense of our churches, it's hard to develop loving relationships in a large church. We have about one thousand families in our church and three different services each weekend. I don't even recognize many of the people who don't go to the service I do. Gathering a small compatible group takes some effort but when people love one another and meet together regularly in the presence of the Holy Spirit, it is a healthy experience and a great benefit to the church and to society.

CHAPTER 8

Sunday School as A Small Prayer Group

It isn't hard being good from time to time in sports. What's tough is being good every day.—Willie Mays

Are you called to help others? Do it with all the strength and energy which God supplies, so God will be glorified.—1 Peter 4:11

I'VE BEEN TEACHING fourth-grade Sunday school at our church for thirty-two years. So I've met with these students almost a thousand times. These ten- and eleven-year-old kids are not yet teenagers, but they can read and write. It's an ideal time to plant seeds of Christianity. They are very intelligent and can understand the basic concepts. In fact they have an advantage over adults. Christ said, "Unless you turn and become as little children, you shall not enter into the kingdom of heaven" (Matthew 18:3). So children can better appreciate the wisdom of Christianity. Their minds are not so much contaminated with biases and a lot of other things as in adults.

Sunday school classes can be as effective as small prayer groups when done in the right way. Each class should begin with a reminder that the Holy Spirit is the same power that caused the dead body of Christ to rise up. (In 1 Peter 3:18, it says, "Christ was put to death in the flesh but was quickened by the spirit.") Also, He is present when people gather in His name in Sunday school. Because the Holy Spirit is present in the classroom, everyone who opens their heart to receive the Spirit feels deep-down peace and joy. When the children do this, classes are lively and have an exuberance that leads to a good time. It's the Holy Spirit that brings people together in love and brings joy to everyone present both in prayer groups and in Sunday school.

When I first started teaching Sunday school, I was told by the director of Religious Education that the previous teacher had trouble with my new class. I just brushed it off thinking my special charismatic approach would be so attractive that I would have no trouble. But children have strong feelings and can be turned off just like adults. A kind of war is the natural result of such a situation. Wars are always destructive, and nothing good comes from them. When people do mean things to each other, everyone loses. I wasn't smart enough or spiritual enough to handle it well. It was a good learning experience. Our natural tendency is to use the parental part of our personality especially when we're supposed to be in charge. My Parent is strong since my mother disciplined her four kids with the broom handle. I did a little yelling in the class, but it did no good. We must stay in the Adult and teach as well as we can under all circumstances. Obviously, in Sunday school as well as in small prayer groups, the parental influence must be kind and gentle and encouraging.

We have an old film-strip projector and tape player in our Sunday school system. The tapes are very good and make good scriptural points and are also entertaining to the children. However, some of the boys think it's funny to wave their arms through the projector light. My response is to move them to seats far enough away from the light so they can't reach it. One of the boys was moved to a place out of reach of the light beam but proceeded to slide his seat desk toward the beam. Two of the girls got out of their seats and gently pushed his seat back where it was. I was so grateful to them. It was one of the most supportive things I've seen in Sunday school, restoring order to the classroom. Girls are generally more mature than boys in the fourth grade.

The boy was a good student and from a nice family, but I'm sure he learned a good lesson that day.

An important part of our fourth-grade Sunday school program at Blessed Sacrament Church is that parents are invited to sit in on the classes each week. They learn what goes on in our classes and are also asked to read important true stories to the class—stories that are hard to explain if there is no God. The children are generally proud to have their parents attend, and the stories are a highlight of the class. Everyone feels good when these stories of modern-day miracles are mentioned. God is not dead, but alive and actively taking care of His people.

CHAPTER 9

Families, Prayer, Faith and Healing

Those who work the hardest, who subject
themselves to the strictest discipline, who give up
certain pleasurable things in order to achieve a
certain goal, are the happiest.—Brutus Hamilton,
Olympic Athlete

FAMILY PROBLEMS ARE common. Several
organizations deal with family problems. The Good
Samaritan Network offers services for families struggling with
poverty of material possessions and poverty of relationships
also. Families First provides people who go to troubled homes
for several weeks to try to teach them how to function well
as a family. This program is successful in maintaining the
normal family structure in 85 percent of the cases for at least
twelve months.

The old saying that "Families that pray together, stay
together" applies here. If families can gather for prayer and,
on a regular basis, open their hearts to God and to each
other, there would be no problem. This presumes that family

members have a deep abiding faith that God hears and answers prayer.

God did not intend that people should live alone. He put us in families. He does all He can to maintain and promote families. One of the most amazing stories of family experiences ever involved a family from Palestine, Texas, visiting their cousins in Houston. The cousins had a swimming pool in their backyard. The visiting family warned their three-year-old not to go to the backyard, but in all the commotion with the two families greeting each other, they lost track of the three-year-old. The mother immediately went to the backyard swimming pool but could see no sign of her son. In a panic, she ran down the street and then back into the house but again did not see her son. Finally she and her niece went to the pool, and they saw something on the bottom of the pool. The niece jumped in and brought up the little boy who by this time had no heartbeat, was not breathing, and was cyanotic. The mother screamed in anguish.

They called 911, and the mother went into the house and prayed that God would save her son. The EMTs were able to get the heart started again, and the mother gave thanks to God and felt everything would be OK. The EMTs rushed the boy to the hospital, but the doctors had bad news. He said that the boy might survive, but if he did, he would probably be paralyzed and severely brain damaged. The mother said no and predicted that he would walk out of the hospital by himself. But at that time, the boy was still on life support systems.

The mother called a local church in Houston and asked for elders to come and pray for her son. He had been unconscious for five days and had developed pneumonia so that the hospital staff thought the end was near. But the mother clung to her faith and anticipated a healing. As the elders prayed for the boy, they noticed that his eyelids fluttered and he wet the bed. His brain was waking up.

The boy walked out of the hospital twenty days later, and seven months after the terrible experience, the doctors pronounced him healthy. The lady thought that since her three-year-old was the youngest of four siblings and was born when she was forty-one years old, God would not take this great family blessing from her. We see that God does not abandon the families He creates. This is especially true when great faith is present.

Another story from *Guideposts* magazine also illustrates that God takes care of families. We need to be reminded of this often. This true story is of a young lady in 1962. She wanted to be a secretary. It was her fondest dream. She saved up from babysitting, and her parents on the dairy farm helped her as much as they could, and she went off to secretarial school. But after a while, she had to drop out of school for lack of funds. She worked hard and got good grades, but now it was over and her dream had faded. She and her family were sad. Her younger brother Jim asked if it was hard to say goodbye to her classmates. She said "Yes, a little" but didn't want to complain.

Jim was an unusual teenager. He was very fond of a cow given to him by his father. The heifer was born on their farm, but the mother cow had died during the birth. Jim named the cow Maxine and took good care of her. He taught her how to drink milk from a bucket and made her a bed of straw in the corner of the barn. Jim rode on Maxine's back like she was a pony. He even slept with the heifer at the county fair because it was the first time Maxine was away from her bed of straw in the barn.

At Christmas, his sister gave Jim a brush for Maxine and said she hoped Maxine would win a ribbon at the county fair next year. Jim, who was fourteen years old, gave his sister an envelope. She thought it would be a Christmas card, but it was a new one-hundred-dollar bill, a lot of money in 1962. The lady ran out into the barn and found Maxine was gone, sold to another farm family who would care for and love her. Jim had given up the cow he loved so much because he loved his sister more. Jim grew up to become a pastor. His sister completed secretarial school and was employed as a secretary for many years. How precious are people who sacrifice themselves for the welfare of their family!

Another true story about faith and family appeared in *Guideposts*, November 1980. A lady in Arlington Heights,

Illinois, woke up one morning feeling very tired. Her husband had already left for work, and her three kids—ages 5, 7, and 9—would be getting up soon. Thank God it was summer. She got up slowly and fell flat on her back. She said to herself, "What a klutz." To get downstairs, she crawled backward down the steps and hoisted herself onto the sofa. She thought this must be a temporary problem. She had always been physically active and was a professional dancer. When the problem persisted, she went to a doctor. Over a period of six months, they did a variety of tests but had trouble coming up with a diagnosis. Finally, they decided she had dermatomyositis. They told her husband Dave that this was a serious disease and in two years she would be in a wheelchair and would live no longer than five years. Also there was no treatment for it. She continued to teach dancing, and her family supported her. Her children helped her with the housework. Her husband worked as a night editor for the *Chicago Tribune* so he could be there for his wife during the day and also when the kids came home. One morning a Bible verse came to her mind: "The joy of the Lord is your strength," Nehemiah 10:8. She always did have trouble remembering Bible verses, but this one stuck with her. She shared it with her husband, and they thought that this was a sign from God that she would be healed, a welcome thought in this desperate situation. However, despite her deep belief, the disease got worse just as the doctor predicted. The lady continued to be hopeful, however, and started teaching her dance classes while lying down. She survived beyond the five-year limit the doctor mentioned.

Church was very important to her, and despite her wheelchair, she went to Sunday services at the local Presbyterian church when possible.

Then eleven years after diagnosis, she had a vision of our Lord in a bluish-white gown. He said she would be healed but asked her to be patient and not to tell anyone yet and to keep using her wheelchair and do what the doctor told her.

A year and a half later, when her recovery was progressing, she shared it with her doctor. She was actually able to stand up and walk, which she had not done in years. The doctor said she was not being healed but this was just a remission and that she would get worse again. He said he had never seen anyone recover from dermatomyositis. But the lady and her family continued to believe that she was being healed. Gradually, she recovered, and six years later, she was completely normal. Deep abiding faith is a powerful thing.

A twelve-year-old boy grew up in Grand Bay, Alabama, and in 1968 was free in the summer since his mom had to work after his father died, and he didn't have to go to school. He and his friend Joel became infamous for their bad behavior. One hot summer afternoon, he and Joel went walking on Old McGregor's farm and discovered a tractor in a shed. They got it started and had fun driving over the planted fields. In the process, they ran down the battery and damaged the gears. The old farmer called the police, and the boy's older sister heard about it and said the farmer knew who did it. The boy called his friend Joel, and they agreed they should talk to Mr. McGregor and confess that they were guilty. So they walked to his farm and knocked on the door. Joel ran off in a panic, and the boy was left alone to face Mr. McGregor. He tearfully related his sins. Mr. McGregor simply said, "I'll pick you up at six on Saturday." So that's what he did every Saturday morning for four years. He paid the boy for all his assistance on the farm mending fences, collecting and burning pecan tree branches, feeding cattle, and cleaning the barn.

Mr. McGregor was an Alabama football fan and would frequently tune in to the games on the radio on Saturday afternoons. The boy became interested in football also and played on his high school team.

With the money he earned from Mr. McGregor and also from working in a shipyard and at a chemical plant, the boy went to college and earned a degree in aerospace engineering. He married and had a son and daughter. He was employed by the Johnson Space Agency and now lives in Houston.

Mr. McGregor did an outstanding community service for this fatherless boy. He taught him responsibility, dedicated service, and helpfulness to others, and enabled him establish his own family and to become an important contributor to society.

These humanitarian efforts of Mr. McGregor are similar to those of Father Flanagan of Boys Town in Omaha, Nebraska, and are sorely needed in society today. In 1917, Father Flanagan established a home for boys who had no families to care for them. He purchased a farm and expanded the program in 1936. The campus in Omaha covers about a hundred acres. Girls were later included, and a concept of family for operation of different households by married couples was established.

In 1938, a movie came out starring Spencer Tracy as Father Flanagan and Mickey Rooney as one of the boys of Boys Town. The movie popularized the whole concept. An Academy Award was given to Spencer Tracy, who later donated the Oscar trophy to Boys Town.

After World War II, President Harry Truman saw the societal value of Father Flanagan's work and encouraged him to go to Asia and Europe to speak about his enterprise. Hopefully he had some positive impact on the people there. But can you believe the people in his home country of Ireland rejected Father Flanagan's idea and continued to deal with problem children with severe discipline just as they did before?

Boys Town centers have now been opened in twelve different sites in the USA, including New York, Florida, Iowa, California, and Washington, DC.

I visited Boys Town in Omaha about ten years ago and was greatly impressed. Although Father Flanagan died in 1948, he made sure his project would live on after him. A series of priests followed Father Flanagan as directors of Boys Town, but the whole program has maintained its interdenominational flavor and is a great blessing to the entire nation and the world.

Father Flanagan made famous the saying, "There is no such thing as a bad boy." He was convinced that these young people could be formed into useful members of society with the proper guidance and encouragement. Throughout the world, Father Edward Flanagan was considered an expert in the area of child development. Pope Pius XI named Father Flanagan a domestic prelate with the title of Right Reverend Monsignor in 1937. He established an organization that continues to do a tremendous job today of saving lost children and allowing them to build strong families.

Small groups of Christians who gather in the name of Jesus feel the power of the Holy Spirit, and it brings great joy. Whether it is Sunday school or a small private group or a family, those who meet to discuss godly things experience the great strength of the Holy Spirit. "Our great power is from God, not from ourselves" (2 Corinthians 4:7). Often families are benefitted by the godly power that comes from prayer groups and from people with a God-oriented perspective like Mr. McGregor and Father Flanagan.

Father Peter Rookey was a famous healing evangelist born the ninth of thirteen children to a strong Catholic family of Irish-French descent in Superior, Wisconsin, in 1916. (See

Heather Parsons. *Man of Miracles*. Blanchardstown, Dublin 15, Ireland: Robert Andrew Press, 1994). His mother, Johanna McGarry, was one of twenty children all born in the USA. She was brought up with a strong sense of Irish identity and Catholic values. Her parents instilled in her a deep belief in the power of God. With their thirteen children, they went to Mass every day and said a family rosary every night.

When he was eight years old, Peter found a giant firecracker on the Fourth of July. Someone had tried to light it, but it didn't work. Peter touched a match to it, but again it didn't explode. He then brought the firecracker close to his mouth and blew on it, and it exploded in his face. As the doctor removed the debris from his face, he told Peter's mother that young Peter would never have his sight again. Peter heard his mother reply, "We'll see about that. From today we'll say a family rosary every day especially for his healing." As they were saying their daily rosaries for him, Peter also prayed that he would receive his eyesight so he could study to become a priest. It took a year and a half, but he finally could see. Thus Peter was given personal evidence that God can indeed perform miracles. Thanks be to God for a strong, faith-filled family that persisted in prayer.

Furthermore, Peter did become a priest, ordained in Chicago, May 17, 1941. He was assigned to duty in the Servite Order and conducted healing services in the USA and in Benburb County, Tyrone, Ireland, for many years. This holy man often fasted all day before he conducted healing services in the evening. Many miraculous healings occurred when Father Rookey prayed for and anointed the sick over a period of about sixty years.

CHAPTER 10

Christianity and Pharmacy

Quality is never and accident. It is always the result of effort.—John Ruskin

Obstacles are those things you see when you take your eyes off your goal.—Hannah More (1845–1933)

PHARMACY IS A fine profession and plays a vital role in health care in our communities throughout the USA and the rest of the world. The pharmacist is well educated in the basic medical sciences pertaining to health care: physiology, pathology, and pharmacology (the three *P*s). Pharmacists are valuable, well-trained advisors to patients in health matters and have a great advantage over other health professionals in that they have free access to the public. If the pharmacist is a deeply spiritual person, they have an opportunity to combine medical science and spirituality and greatly benefit people in need of healing.

I taught pharmacology to pharmacy students for forty-five years and also was faculty advisor to a student prayer group at Purdue College of Pharmacy for sixteen years. This is an important group in our College of Pharmacy. If we can deepen the spirituality of just a few of our students and enhance their ability to share concepts of divine healing, we can greatly enhance quality of pharmacy practice for years to come.

We mentioned that people who are deeply spiritual live longer than those who do not go to church. The pharmacist can share his or her strong spiritual attitudes along with sound health information and present a coherent spiritual and scientific message so that miracles can happen.

Our group was started in 1996 when a few students led by a fine Christian pharmacy student named Kristine Overley met informally with a few of her fellow students to discuss the Bible and relate it to the profession of pharmacy. There was an open, honest atmosphere there where everyone admitted a great need for God in their lives. They recognized the great spiritual need for pharmacists to become maximally effective.

After Kristine graduated, our group leader Jean Ann Custis thought we should be recognized by Purdue University, so she filled out the necessary forms and submitted them. The university accepted and approved our application, and we became a legitimate student organization of Purdue in October 2002.

In 2006, our president Cory Smith applied for membership in CPFI (Christian Pharmacists' Fellowship International), and we were accepted as a student chapter. The mission of CPFI is to promote spiritual growth and fellowship for like-minded professionals and integration of faith with the practice of pharmacy. The national office is in West Palm Beach, Florida, on the campus of a university.

A custom we tried to perpetuate in our group was prayer with the group president and the faculty advisor just before each weekly meeting to invite the Holy Spirit to guide the meeting and inspire each one who attends. Also before the beginning of the school year in August, our group president and faculty advisor would meet with really good Christians on the Purdue campus to ask for their prayers for us as we began the new school year. We realized that we could not conduct these meetings on our own. Without the help of the Holy Spirit, we knew our group would be ineffective.

The above procedure worked well for many years, and it was a good thing for our pharmacy college. We looked forward to our weekly meetings. However a new group of students decided that they did not need a strong charismatic influence and did not need to meet frequently. The group went through a dry period and concluded that it was only when we can forgive others and allow God's atonement to melt the strong feelings of resentment in our frozen hearts that the Holy Spirit can work through us to build the kingdom in a powerful way and allow us to be maximally effective as pharmacists.

Pharmacists have to work with sick people, and often it's not easy. Don Brown was head of our student pharmacy at Purdue for many years. He said it was a lot easier to deal with young students than it was to work in community pharmacy where you have to deal with grouchy old people. Some sick older people would make Don so angry he wished they would never come into his store again.

So there is a great need for pharmacists to be deeply spiritual and to be able to overlook offences and help people as best they can. Pharmacy students need to meet regularly with each other to deepen their Christian spirituality and be prepared for all the stresses and strains of a demanding profession. They need to hear regularly stories of how God intervenes in the lives of people devoted to Him. Strong Christian fellowship among pharmacy students is important to prepare them for the rigors of professional pharmacy.

Can I please share a story about a pharmacy student I counseled and how important God is in the personal lives of these students? I've counseled many students over the years, but this one stands out in my mind. He was very fond of a young lady pharmacy student in his class, but she didn't respond favorably to him. He was beside himself when he came to talk to me. He came from a family that did not go to church. He was doing well enough in school but was a little edgy as you might expect under the circumstances. I mentioned to him (as I did to many other students) that we humans are tripartite in nature, with a body, mind, and spirit, and all three parts need to be fed. We eat breakfast, lunch, and dinner to keep our bodies well-nourished and in pharmacy school, student's minds get overloaded usually. However, our spirits need also to be fed, and I suggested to this student that his spirit was extremely malnourished. His girlfriend, by contrast, was a devout Catholic. What I said made sense to this young man, and he started going to church and became deeply spiritual himself. About a year later, he married his girlfriend. They now have several children, and both have successful careers in pharmacy. The Holy Spirit can work powerfully in relationships and build strong families and strong Christian pharmacists.

CHAPTER 11

Drug Abuse, Society and Religion

The foundation of excellence lies in self-control.
—H. L. Baugher

We are half-hearted creatures fooling about with drink and sex and ambition when infinite joy is offered to us.—C. S. Lewis

TO HAVE A well-ordered productive society, we need to minimize drug abuse. A commonly abused chemical is ethanol, which is perfectly legal in the USA and in many other countries as well. Yet it causes a severe addiction in 10 percent of its users. People addicted to ethanol usually die from the effects of the drug.

Yet when people become severely addicted to ethanol, God still does not abandon them. In fact, the only really effective treatment of this lethal addiction to ethanol is Alcoholics Anonymous. One of the twelve steps in this program is belief in a higher power. No matter how intelligent or how strong-willed people are, they cannot overcome alcoholism by themselves. Drugs are not effective; psychiatrists really do not help. People must have faith in a higher power to overcome strong alcohol addiction. Severe alcoholism is a death sentence, and the only sure cure is the twelve-step program and help from God.

There is a strong movement today in the USA to legalize marijuana. Use of recreational and medicinal marijuana is now legal in Alaska, Colorado, Oregon, and in Washington, DC, as of the year 2016. People think that marijuana is not harmful and has good medicinal effects. They forget that about 10 percent of the people who use marijuana become addicted, and this leads to abuse of ethanol and heroin.

Marijuana is of some value in reduction of nausea and vomiting after chemotherapy, improvement of appetite in HIV/AIDS, and in cigarette-smoking cessation. But there are already other drugs that can also be used for these indications.

Marijuana is said to be the most popular drug of abuse with 181 million users worldwide. This is compared to 33 million users of amphetamine and about the same number of opioid abusers worldwide.

Recently a young associate professor from Columbia University, Carl Hart, spoke at Purdue on promoting social justice through a neuropsychopharmacology lens. He mentioned some drugs of abuse lead to incarceration of mainly African Americans. This is true of crack cocaine, in which 80 percent of those arrested are African Americans.

It's a form of racial discrimination. Dr. Hart said that these drugs really do not have bad side effects and that people can function normally despite using drugs. He claimed that the mayor of Washington, DC, and presidents Obama, Bush, and Clinton all took some drugs of abuse and still functioned relatively normally. He was asked about ethanol in his lecture at Purdue, and he said its side effects were minimal. He further stated that we need ethanol to help people loosen up—especially around universities, which have many boring meetings. He also thought that legalizing marijuana was a good idea.

Despite what Dr. Hart said, ethanol is a destructive drug and causes harm to self or others in seventy percent of those who abuse it. Liver cirrhosis and fetal alcohol syndrome are two of the most serious side effects of ethanol. About two-thirds of the population of the USA uses ethanol, and ten percent of these people become addicted. Yet the use of ethanol is still legal. Now we are in the process of legalizing marijuana, which also produces addiction in ten percent of users. Seems to me this is a trend that is going in the wrong direction.

Marijuana impairs mental acuity, memory, attention, reduces alertness, and impairs judgment.

Drugs are needed for certain disease states and can do a lot of good, but side effects can also occur. Side effects are especially common with psychoactive agents. The many drugs that act on the brain—sedatives, hypnotics, tranquilizers—are not specific. They alter brain functions beyond those desired in therapy. Dr. Tom Miya, who hired me here at Purdue and was head of Pharmacology, said, "It's best not to take any drugs at all." They alter the fine-tuning of delicate systems of the body.

We said the human brain is complex, having twelve billion interconnecting neurons. God set up this system to function ideally. If you put drugs into the system, you risk disturbing the balance and causing problems.

One critical process for health is sleep. Tissue repair occurs during sleep, and if we disturb sleep, tissue repair does not occur normally. So taking drugs may alter sleep and prevent healing of tissue damage that normally occurs during everyday activity in blood vessels, skeletal muscle, skin, and other tissues.

Caffeine is not severely addictive like ethanol or marijuana, but it is the most widely used psychoactive substance in the world. Ninety percent of the people in North America use caffeine every day. Also, some people become addicted to caffeine and are unable to decrease use even when aware of bad health effects. A cup of coffee has about one hundred milligrams of caffeine and Classic Coke thirty-four milligrams. A toxic dose is one thousand milligrams. Toxic symptoms are fidgeting, anxiety, and rambling flow of thought or speech. Caffeine blocks adenosine receptors in the brain and blocks the tired feeling that helps us go to sleep at night. That's why drinking coffee late at night causes insomnia. Also, some people are more sensitive to caffeine than others. Although caffeine addiction is not a major societal problem, those who are hypersensitive to it should avoid caffeine intake.

CHAPTER 12

Mental Illness as A Disturbance in Society

The human body experiences a powerful gravitational pull in the direction of hope.
—Norman Cousins

D RUGS DO HAVE side effects. It's best not to take any drugs if you do not have to. However, they can also be extremely useful. A problem of major proportions present in our world today is mental illness. We each need to be aware of it in the people around us. Schizophrenia occurs in about 0.5 percent of the world population, or in 23.6 million people globally. However, that includes only people actually diagnosed with the disease. Donna Fox, program director of National Alliance for Mental Illness (NAMI) for the State of Minnesota, says that the true incidence of schizophrenia is 20 percent. That's one fifth of the population!

Many people with schizophrenia cannot hold a job and must be taken care of by others. Thus many families are affected by mental illness. Psychoses are the third most common disabling condition after quadriplegia and dementia. So this is a serious problem in society today. It affects men and women equally and occurs in similar rates in all ethnic groups. NAMI is a much-needed charitable organization in the USA dedicated to helping people with mental illness. NAMI has mobile crisis teams that are able to quickly give aid to anyone who asks for help. A problem here is that so many of these mentally ill people think they don't need help. This is called anosognosia.

Symptoms of schizophrenia are disorganized thinking and speech (word salad), social withdrawal, sloppiness of dress and hygiene, loss of motivation and judgment, and sometimes paranoia and hoarding useless things. Some may be schizoid and have some but not all of the symptoms. Schizoaffective disorder also includes psychic depression. Living in an urban environment increases the incidence of schizophrenia by a factor of two. Regular exercise has a positive mental and physical effect on those who have schizophrenia. Early exposure to marijuana is strongly associated with an increased risk of mental illness two to three times. Amphetamine worsens psychotic symptoms. Caffeine addiction is common in schizophrenia. There is a marked increased incidence of smoking cigarettes from 20 percent in the normal population to 85 percent in schizophrenics. Mental illness decreases life span by ten to twenty-five years. Suicide occurs in 5 percent of these people. Despite all this, many people with mental illness can lead rewarding and meaningful lives in their communities with the proper care. We need to mention three important approaches to treatment of mental illness: drugs, counseling, and prayer.

Xavier Amador, a PhD in psychology, wrote a book, *I Am Not Sick, I Don't Need Help!* (1150 Smith Road, Peconic, New York: Vida Press, 2012). The book deals with treatment of mental illness with drugs. He makes two main points in the book. First, people with schizophrenia have altered nerve tracts in their brains and do not perceive that they are ill (anosognosia). They believe they don't need to take drugs. Second, if they can be convinced that they need to take drugs regularly, drugs can prevent worsening of mental illness!

Schizophrenia has both positive and negative symptoms. Disordered thoughts and speech and also visual hallucinations are positive symptoms that respond well to drug therapy. Negative symptoms include lack of emotion, poverty of speech, inability to experience pleasure (anhedonia), and lack of desire to form relationships. Negative symptoms do not respond well to drug therapy and are more of a burden to other people.

Deficits can occur in attention or memory. Verbal memory impairment is linked to a problem in processing information. Healthy people remember positive words better (Pollyanna principle). Schizophrenics remember all words equally well and are at a disadvantage.

Providing instructions for these people improves function. Training emphasizes repeated verbalization of tasks and giving encouraging coping instructions to self to handle failure. In other words these people are just like the rest of us. They have to work at it and keep a positive attitude to accomplish anything.

Fortunately, cognitive ability is stable and does not deteriorate over time in contrast to other problems in schizophrenia. Counseling aims to change the patient's thinking to be more adaptive and healthy and build on their cognitive ability to improve behavior.

When the antipsychotic drug chlorpromazine came out in the mid-1950s, many mental hospitals built the previous seventy-five years were closed. Using this drug allowed schizophrenics to leave the rigid confines of an asylum and return to the comfort of their own homes and communities. What a blessing this drug was for many families and to our society!

Side effects are always a risk when drugs are used. These antipsychotic drugs may cause stiff motor movements in walking and posture. Quetiapine (Seroquel) causes less abnormal muscle function but may cause some weight gain and diabetic symptoms.

Like any illness, schizophrenia can have a physical cause, or it may be caused by demonic possession. Remember the woman from Canaan who cried out to Jesus "Have mercy on me O Lord, Son of David! My daughter is severely demon possessed" (Matthew 15:22). The disciples said, "Send her away saying she cries out after us." Jesus then said, "I was not sent except for the lost sheep of Israel." Then the woman said "Lord please help me." Jesus answered, "It is not good to take the children's bread and throw it to little dogs." She said, "Yes Lord even the little dogs eat the crumbs from the master's table." Jesus then said, "O woman great is your faith, let it be as you desire," and her daughter was healed at that very hour (Matthew 15: 22–28). Jesus showed that He had power over the demon that possessed the little girl. However the NAMI people believe that mental illness has only a biological origin despite what the Bible says. The following modern story indicates that mental illness can be a spiritual problem.

Power over the evil spirit of mental illness was shown in the ministry of a priest we mentioned before, Father Peter Rookey. In 1992, a lady suffering from psychic depression for four years went to a healing service conducted by Father Peter at a church in Doyleston, Pennsylvania. During the first two years of her illness she was able to function, but during the last two years, the depression was so severe that she was dysfunctional. Then when Father Rookey prayed for her, she was "slain in the Spirit" (fell to the floor and lay semiconscious). She could see scenes from the past and felt God's love and healing. He continued to pray for her, and she felt sick physically. Her body contorted uncontrollably.

Her tongue came out of her mouth, and her eyes rolled back in her head. She could hear her mother crying. When Father Rookey blessed her with the crucifix, anger would well up within her, and she would scream wildly. It was an awful and scary experience. People gave her holy water to drink, and she started to throw up and to curse. All these responses were uncontrollable.

Then she felt she could control her legs, but her arm was controlled by a "magnetic force," and she would make a fist and swing at Father Peter. She also spat at Father and at the crucifix. However, Father Peter continued to pray for almost four hours, and she finally came to her senses and felt a large improvement in emotional health.

Father Peter invited her to come the next day to another healing service in a church in New Jersey. After she took the Eucharist, her face and hands began to burn. After Mass, she went up to the altar of Mary and asked for a sign that she was healed. She detected a strong odor of roses. Father Peter again prayed for her, and she again detected a strong odor of roses. She knew then that she had received sufficient grace to be healed.

Father Rookey explains that we are all constantly attacked by evil spirits. He tells the story of a girl from Atlanta, Georgia, brought to him by her anxious parents. The father was Jewish and her mother was Catholic. The girl herself had been involved with the occult and had given herself to Wicca, the witch, in exchange for certain powers that she listed for Father Peter. Father challenged her to pit those powers against the powers of Christ. The girl said no, and that she was happy that the witch had given her those powers. Father continued to urge the girl to match those powers with the power of Christ but she refused and ran away crying to sit in the car outside.

The next time Father Rookey was in Atlanta, he visited the parents, who by this time had committed the girl to an expensive mental hospital. The girl did not like the hospital and invited Father Peter to visit her. She was now open to exorcism, but Father Rookey doubted that the doctors would approve his visit. However, the clinical staff allowed him to come. The exorcism took some time, but the powers of Wicca were no match for the powers of Christ. Before Father Peter left, he and the girl said a rosary together. Her life was turned around. She and her boyfriend (who was also involved with Wicca) started going to Mass together.

Without proper therapy, mental illness worsens. Thinking becomes less clear, hygiene more slovenly, and hallucinations more common. Yet mentally ill people believe they are not sick and don't need treatment. For adults to be treated, these people must request help from professionals despite their convictions that they don't need help. This is a huge roadblock in bringing people to receive treatment they really need.

If they are suicidal or violent toward others, the police can be called. Many departments have crisis intervention teams (CIT) that include people trained to deal with these situations and who can distinguish between criminal behavior and mental illness.

Also, most hospitals have psychiatric care units and mobile crisis teams that can refer patients to the hospital or can arrange for outpatient treatment.

CHAPTER 13

Conclusion

And let us with caution indulge the supposition that morality can be maintained without religion. —George Washington

The Christian ideal has not been tried and found wanting; it has been found difficult and left untried.—G. K. Chesterton

I T HAS BEEN a great joy for me to meet with two fine, intelligent pharmacy students from Vietnam. When the Christian pharmacy students reduced the frequency of our meeting times, Phu Vo and his girlfriend, Nhu Phamn, were the only ones who understood the importance meeting often and of following the guidance of the Holy Spirit. Phu had spent some time in Seattle, Washington, while in the process of applying for admission to our College of Pharmacy. In Seattle, he was introduced to Christianity and was baptized in the Holy Spirit. I was greatly impressed with his sincerity and honesty. We have been meeting frequently now for about two years, and only recently did he reveal his experience with the Spirit. I'm grateful that I was able to recognize the validity of his spirituality early on. The Holy Spirit does indeed leave a recognizable mark on people who have opened their hearts to Him and are firmly grounded in Christ and born again.

The Purdue Christian Pharmacy Student Association meets less often, but they are still meeting. I pray for them and hope they fulfill the original purpose of the group. I believe that our organization will have a good long-lasting influence on the profession of pharmacy through my friends Phu and Nhu and all the other Spirit-filled students who have attended.

In the Nuremberg trials for crimes committed in World War II, those responsible for the deaths of many people argued that what they did was perfectly legal in their nation. They were only following orders. However they were found guilty of crimes against humanity. A nation's laws must be just and godly and not the opinions of men. Ultimately, we are all responsible to God, and ungodly laws cannot protect us.

Isn't it ironic that we in the USA are now going against godly ways by approving abortion and same-sex marriage? Aren't we as guilty as those Nazi leaders in violating godly laws? In pharmacy we work diligently to develop new drugs to cure cancer or relieve headaches, but we mostly ignore the thousands of healthy, innocent babies who lose their lives to abortion every day. How can this be? Pope John Paul II said the nation that sacrifices its own children has no future. God have mercy on us. May He take away our blindness so we can see our sins and can repent and change our ways.

Strong healthy families are the foundation of good societies. We need to do everything we can to strengthen family ties. Both a fatherly and a motherly influence are important. We already mentioned that we do what we can to strengthen families in our Sunday school program at Blessed Sacrament Church. Parents attend each class. It makes the kids feel good when their parents come, and we say a special prayer for the family of the parent who attends the class.

We should emphasize again the tremendous power of the Holy Spirit. When we are filled with strong faith and with the power of the Holy Spirit, all things are possible. That same Spirit can dwell in us and enliven and encourage us to intercede for miracles in our efforts to build the kingdom of God here on earth.

Dick Westley was a philosophy professor at Loyola University and had much experience with small prayer groups. In his book (*Good Things Happen: Experiencing Community in Small Groups.* Mystic, Connecticut: Twenty-Third Publications, 1992) he makes the following points.

"Christianity is dependent on how well we fellowship with other people. Small prayer groups provide a means by which we get to know each other and develop loving relationships. Great benefits come when we belong to a healthy small prayer group. Only then can we be ourselves, achieve true freedom and attain salvation. In the absence of a loving community our institutional church becomes a 'formalistic travesty.' In summary, good small prayer groups are vital for the ultimate meaning of human life and Christian faith."

These words were written twenty-five years ago but are more relevant today than ever. We humans must be part of a group of people united with God and especially His Holy Spirit. The future of our entire civilization depends upon our ability to form effective small groups to share our faith in God with people around us.

Small charismatic prayer groups do not detract from traditional church services. For example, the Catholic Mass is a powerful ritual and a very holy process. Mass is celebrated somewhere around the world every moment of every day except Good Friday. Both small prayer groups and church services honor God and serve to build the kingdom.

Father Richard Rohr, a Franciscan priest, has emphasized Trinity as a concept of God in his new book *Divine Dance* (1030 Hunt Valley Circle, New Kensington, Pennsylvania 15068: Whitaker House, 2016). Contrary to what it says in Wikipedia, God has never been a lonesome creature sitting on a throne in heaven. God is a relationship. He loves His eternal Son, Jesus. That great love between them is also a Person, the Holy Spirit. There is perfect harmony among this Trinity. Never is there anything but absolute agreement and perfect justice in this holy group. Thus God is a Holy Community, but that community is not exclusive. There's room for us also to become partakers in that relationship. Jesus had to endure the Passion and die on the cross to atone for our sins and make us worthy to be companions of the Holy Trinity. But forgiveness is not automatic. We need the power and strength of that blood on the cross to make forgiveness a reality even when our hearts are broken and we are crushed in spirit. Thank you, Jesus, for the enormous love that allowed you to make that great sacrifice for us. Help us to enter that divine dance totally as we do our best to build the kingdom of God here on earth.

May God the Father, Son, and Holy Spirit be forever adored and glorified by civilizations everywhere.

INDEX

A

abortion, 2, 6, 20, 41, 96
Abraham (patriarch), 14–15
Adult. *See under* personality
alcoholism, 81–82
Amador, Xavier, 89

B

barber, 6–7
Berne, Eric, 43, 49
Bleier, Rocky, 34–35
Boys Town, 70–71

C

caffeine, 84–85, 88
Child. *See under* personality
chlorpromazine, 90
Constitution of the United States,
    20–21, 23–24
CPFI (Christian Pharmacists'
    Fellowship International), 77
crucifixion, 4
Custis, Jean Ann, 76

D

dermatomyositis, 67–68
Divine Dance (Rohr), 98

E

ethanol, 81–84
EU (European Union), 29–32

F

families, 14, 31, 35, 45, 47–48, 57,
    61, 63–71, 78–79, 87, 90, 97
FGBFI (Full Gospel Businessmen's
    Fellowship International),
    54–55
Flanagan, Edward, 70–71
free will, 3–4, 6, 11
French Revolution, 25–26

G

Games People Play (Berne), 43, 49
government, vii–viii, 19–26,
    30–31
Guandolo, John, 5

H

Harris, Thomas, 49–50
Hart, Carl, 82–83
Holy Roman Empire, 24–25, 29
Holy Spirit, ix, 4, 15, 55–57, 60, 71, 77, 79, 95–99

I

I Am Not Sick, I Don't Need Help! (Amador), 89
I'm OK, You're OK (Harris), 49, 51
Islam, 5, 27–29

J

Jim (teenager with cow), 66

K

Khrushchev, Nikita, 50

L

Lincoln, Abraham, 21–22, 32, 53, 56

M

MADD (Mothers Against Drunk Drivers), 39
manic depression, 48
marijuana, 82–84, 88
McGregor (farmer), 68–71
Melchizedek (king of Salem), 14–15, 17
mental illness, 87–89, 91, 93–94
Mohammed (prophet of Islam), 5, 27–29

N

NAMI (National Alliance for Mental Illness), 87–88, 91
"not OK" Child, 49–50

O

Overley, Kristine, 76

P

PAC construct, 45–49
Parent. *See under* personality
passive aggression, 46
Paul, Saint (the apostle), 33, 53–54
personality
   Adult, 44–51, 61
   Child, 44–50
   Parent, 44–50, 60
pharmacists, 75–76, 78
pharmacy, 75–79, 95–96
philosophers, 17
pontifex maximus, 17–18
prophets, 15–17, 27–28
purgatory, 10–11

R

Rohr, Richard, 98
Rookey, Peter, 71–73, 91–93

S

same-sex marriage, 20, 25, 41, 96
San Quentin (prison), 36–38
schizophrenia, 87–90
Small Prayer Groups, ix, 53, 55–56, 59–61, 97–98

Smith, Earl, 36–38
Socrates (philosopher), 16–17
Sunday school, 59–61, 71, 97

T

transaction, 44–46
transactional analysis, ix, 45
Trinity, 55, 98–99
Trump, Donald, 23–24

U

undertaker, 35

W

Western Roman Empire, 26
Wiesel, Elie, 5

CPSIA information can be obtained
at www.ICGtesting.com
Printed in the USA
FFHW021839030119
50050827-54843FF